Jesus Not Me-sus

COPYRIGHT © Dr. Danny Griffin,
1st Edition May 2019
Printed in the United States of America

Dr. Danny Griffin
dwadegriffin@gmail.com
www.SpiritualMaintenance.org

DEDICATION

This book is dedicated to the hundreds of loving, caring men and women of all ages and backgrounds who have loved and prayed for me without judgement over the years. Your patience set me free to grow in grace allowing the Holy Spirit to address my life through the good, bad and ugly of my journey. You all have blessed my life and I am grateful! It is indeed about JESUS NOT ME-SUS! LOVE AND PRAYERS TO ALL!

SPECIAL DEDICATION

This book I dedicate to my son Lieutenant Governor of Arkansas, Tim Griffin. He has been a constant source of encouragement and blessing! I also appreciate his military service and love for our country. A faithful son, husband, father and public servant that I dearly love!

Table of Contents

INTRODUCTION

THE WORD HERO MEANS DIFFERENT THINGS TO DIFFERENT PEOPLE. I USE HERO IN RELATIONSHIP TO ORDINARY PEOPLE WHO HAVE PUT GOD'S LOVE AND GRACE INTO SHOE LEATHER IN THIS BROKEN WORLD THUS BRINGING INTO OUR LIVES A SPIRITUAL NOBILITY EMPOWERED BY THE SPIRIT OF GOD, MAKING A DIFFERENCE. THERE ARE MANY AMONG US WHOSE DEEDS OF KINDNESS AND QUIET, FAITHFUL SERVICE ARE BY THIS STANDARD HEROIC TO GOD'S GLORY AND OUR GOOD. THE SCRIPTURE COMMANDS US, "MAINTAIN GOOD WORKS FOR THEY ARE PROFITABLE TO MANKIND." OTHERS SEEING OUR GOOD WORKS, "GLORIFY THE FATHER WHICH IS IN HEAVEN." AS BELIEVERS WE MUST BE REAL IN OUR "FAITH WALK." THESE ARE TROUBLED TIMES AND OUR IDENTITY WITH JESUS CHRIST WILL BE DECLARED BY WHO WE ARE AND HOW WE LIVE RATHER THAN BY A LIST OF DO'S AND DON'TS, OR GOD TALK. JESUS, NOT ME-SUS, IS THE "AUTHOR AND FINISHER OF OUR FAITH!" IT IS A RELATIONSHIP WITH GOD, "IN CHRIST" NOT RELIGION!

WALK WITH ME THROUGH THE FOLLOWING SALVATION DRAMA IN FIVE ACTS!

ACT 1

We humans are the only creatures on earth who spend hours viewing our behavior or reading about and contemplating it by way of TV, theater and the printed word! Viewing the behavior of others reveals our deep curiosity about the good, the bad and ugly of our lives. I have manifested such behaviors over my lifetime. The gift of "God's righteousness" according to Scripture is our salvation. I have no righteousness of my own, for my nature is to serve my own self-interest!

The "I" in the middle of the word sin is at the core of my brokenness and rebellion. I desire to answer to no one, "FRANKLY I DON'T GIVE A DAMN," reflects my ME-SUS core. I am entertained by reading and viewing human behavior of every variety. Deep inside I hunger for that which would realign my life and values, knowing I am broken.

JESUS CHRIST was just a good man that was to help me be good. This was my initial response. I soon discovered that this would not work. Then into my moral and religious fog came the simple message of God's Grace. Jesus Christ, born of a virgin, lived a sinless life, died on the cross for my sin and rose from the dead. This was a reality, offering me a pardon for my sin debt. My response was a reach in the dark, introducing me to a peace and a joy I had never known, giving me the GIFT OF HIS RIGHTEOUSNESS!

For the first time in my life I desired accountability and discovered a growing love and respect for others I had never known. Reading about and viewing human behavior caused me now to see the rift between God and man! The Bible became a different book causing me to see for the first time the warts and brokenness of its characters. Bible Study is the BS that made the difference. THE BIBLE CHARACTERS WERE JUST LIKE ME AND GOD LOVED THEM AND DESIRED FOR THEM TO FULFILL HIS PLAN AND PURPOSE! God also turns us over to ourselves and our choices to face the penalty of our choices.

Jesus didn't come into the world to DAMN OR CONDEMN IT, BUT TO REDEEM IT! Jesus did not come to rain on OUR parade but set US FREE TO BE A CONDUIT OF GOD'S LOVE AND FORGIVENESS WITH HOPE AND HELP! Now what I read and what I view is always through the prism of GOD'S LOVE AND GRACE. Mankind with his ability to choose lives APART from that grace, self-condemned. JESUS FREELY BOUGHT AND PAID FOR THE GIFT OF GOD'S RIGHTEOUSNESS! WE CHOOSE TO RECEIVE THAT GIFT, BECOMING A HIGHLY FAVORED, IMPERFECT BUT FORGIVEN CHILD OF GOD! IT'S NOT ABOUT RELIGION BUT A RELATION-SHIP! JESUS NOT ME-SUS!

ACT 2

TEAM JESUS: Competition is not in itself evil and can accomplish good, but as anything else mankind touches; it can do great harm and become painful. In the arena of sports, competition is a driving force and can produce excellence and develop strong character as it creates challenges and adversity. For those of us who view competition as fans, it becomes a great source of entertainment and common interest. The down side is that it can become a religion, creating fanaticism, anger and even hurt.

I played drums in a marching band in High School, traveling and playing at football games with great excitement and pride in our team. Team spirit in human competition is great fun and can solidify community and friendships. On youth trips over the years we divided into teams for duties, skits and sports, creating competition and fun with the objective of winning and being "the better TEAM".

The dark side of "TEAM SPIRIT" and competition when applied to our spiritual journey can create a self-righteous divisive behavior and be self-defeating, even painful. Scripture declares that as believers we should not compare ourselves with others, thus being "without understanding." The tragedy of "we alone got it right" as believers is the creator of hundreds of divisions, denominations and error.

Looking to JESUS alone as the AUTHOR and FINISHER of our faith, the only MEDIATOR between God and man and the FIRST AND THE LAST, brings HOPE and REDEMPTION to us all. CALLED OUT ONES is what the BODY OF CHRIST is all about and composes our REDEEMED TEAM (our oneness in Christ). Thus, in our FAITH JOURNEY we are in competition with no one. As followers of a sports team we desire that they win and be the best. TEAM JESUS is not a competitive team but a people FOUND and CALLED OUT for GOD'S purpose of world REDEMPTION.

We all have sinned and "missed the mark" and God fulfilled His promise to provide salvation for all who would believe. JESUS, the "Lamb of God," came to die on the Cross, be BURIED and ROSE from the dead for the sin debt of the world. The sacrifices of the Old Testament were shadows of what was to come.

The word TEAM includes those of LIKE TRUST, who walk together with the same mind. The word CHURCH is not a place, a piece of real estate, a building made with hands, or a human design, but a people CALLED OF GOD TO RECEIVE. THE PROVISION OF HIS RIGHTEOUSNESS IS NOT BASED ON OUR PERFORMANCE. UNDER THE OLD COVENANT MAN'S SALVATION WAS BASED ON BELIEVING GOD'S PROMISE, BUT IN THE NEW COVENANT MAN IS TO BELIEVE "WHOM

GOD SENT" TO FULFILL THAT PROMISE. THIS ALLOWS US TO RECEIVE THE GIFT OF HIS RIGHTEOUSNESS.
JESUS COMMISSIONED US AS BELIEVERS FROM THE TIME OF HIS RESURRECTION TO GO INTO ALL THE WORLD AND PROCLAIM THE GOOD NEWS OF HIS MISSION AND MESSAGE, DISCIPLING THE NATIONS. THUS WE WHO ARE THE CHURCH (TEAM JESUS); PROCLAIM HE ALONE IS KING OF KINGS AND LORD OF LORDS. WE ARE ALL ONE BODY FOR EVER AND EVER WITHOUT COMPETITION OR DIVISION. JESUS CHRIST WAS BORN IN POVERTY, DIED IN PAIN, AGONY AND DISGRACE, DYING ON A "RUGGED CROSS" FOR US. THUS, LOVE IS GRACE'S FREE GIFT!

So much of my spiritual growth has come through the struggle with bad choices, missed opportunities, confused thinking, thoughtlessness, selfishness, and my old sin nature which caused me PAIN! Suffering gets our attention and causes us to listen with our inner ears, addressing our inner man. Suffering or affliction, as it is often called in the Scriptures, gives us the ability to help others in their affliction. As believers we know that God is touched by our infirmities.

Trials can make you stronger. Sorrow reminds us that we are human. Failure can humble us. The Scriptures deal with the nature and character of God who loves and cares for mankind. The journey from Adam and Eve to Noah, to Abraham, to Moses, to David and eventually Jesus Christ is filled with FAITH and FAILURE. GOD uses OUR PAIN AND SUFFERING to His glory and for our good. Thus situations, difficulties and failures at a moment in time may produce hurt, pain and suffering that eventually produces blessing and spiritual growth. It is about JESUS NOT ME-SUS!

ACT 3

The clock said 3:00 AM an hour earlier than my usual JOURNEY INVENTORY & REVIEW TIME! I recalled this morning how disappointed some "brothers & sisters in the Lord" have been in me when my humanity sprung a leak. They were still friendly to my face but held me at arm's length because I did not meet their expectations.

I thought, if they only knew about me what God knows about me, they really would "freak out"! My favorite of men in the OT was David the "SHEPHERD KING OF ISRAEL, A MAN AFTER GOD'S OWN HEART"! Adultery, deceit, lying, betrayal, murder and finally repentance revealed his humanity and his capacity for sin. His poetry addresses my life daily as I embrace his words! His family also revealed brokenness and failure as do all our families. From incest to treason, and murder, his family's humanity leaked. Finally, his son Solomon, a man of great wisdom and the third king of Israel revealed as he aged a major leak in his humanity! With his 700 wives, 300 mistresses and excesses of every kind, God divided Israel!

We are talking SOAP OPERA TIME! The hard reality is that GOD'S WONDERFUL GRACE DOES NOT REMOVE OUR MANIFEST HUMANITY IN THIS LIFE NOR DOES IT EXCUSE IT, BUT HE KEEP LOVING US WHILE HATING OUR SIN AND ALLOWING US

TO PAY THE PRICE FOR OUR CHOICES! Thus, those believers who choose to hold us at arm's length because we do not meet their spiritual expectations only reveal their own insecurities, immaturity and lack of humility. Sooner or later our inability and our leaky, sinful humanity will surface and we all will declare in our repentance, "AMAZING GRACE, HOW SWEET THE SOUND, THAT SAVED A WRETCH LIKE ME"! Each believer in Jesus Christ is on a personal journey with each person at a different place, with different issues, yet with like struggles and suffering!

No agreement necessary! The fight over agreement often leads to a "keep face" ego war! Argument and debate is not involved, but searching the Scriptures to see if they are so. Thus, we give the Holy Spirit an opportunity to do His work in "God's time" without brain washing each other with a "cookie cutter" mentality. Who we believe is the issue more than what we believe. When the Who is established as our final authority, what we believe grows out of that authority.

Humility is the mark of a maturing believer. True intimacy develops in a one on one in your face relationship to allow each to face the other, making a connection with the person addressed. Time together is absolutely essential. Find time, make time and take time to share your hearts, mind and soul without fear of disclosure or intimidation. "Where two or three are gathered together in my name, **THERE AM I** in the midst of them," said JESUS! The believer's spiritual growth and development demands intimacy, the very heart of nurture.

As I look back over the years it appears too much time has been spent on real estate, buildings, monies and numbers. Each believer craves at some point intimacy, an opportunity to ask questions and question answers. Somehow we have often just taken it for granted that it is normal to just buy into a routine that offers very little space for "searching out the Scriptures to see if they are so," in an environment of love without dogma and judgment. It is the Holy Spirit alone who came to "convict the world of sin, righteousness and judgment," and none of that has our signature on it. Thus, as we believers grow in grace and knowledge, humility allows the manifestation of God's grace, by "bearing one another's burden and fulfilling the law of Christ."

Every believer is equal to the other and we each have different gifts to manifest in the body of Christ. We have created too often a caste system with "preachers on top" along with different "religious orders" down the chain to the regular "pew Christian". This is nonsense as we are all equal with different gifts but the same relation to God as His children. God Has No Pets! Each of us has the same challenge and authority as called of God, imperfect, sinful, undeserving, but redeemed, forgiven and greatly blessed children of God.

The Scriptures are for each of us equally and they alone our teacher. Thus, we must seek out intimacy with others who will abide by the need to be real and honest, sharing our hunger. Talking heads and faceless crowds will never produce intimacy. Sitting in pews back to back will never do more than allow us to be distracted by hair styles, clothes, ears and rears, head shapes, and bodies. Lectures and sermons can indeed evangelize with a clear message but growth and nurture demands "face to face" sharing. THE HOLY SPIRIT IS OUR PRIMARY TEACHER WHEREAS WE BELIEVERS ARE GIFTED TO BRING FORWARD SCRIPTURE TO ONE ANOTHER SO THAT THE HOLY SPIRIT CAN AND WILL DO HIS PERFECT WORK IN GOD'S TIME. JESUS NOT ME-SUS!

ACT 4

FEEDING OUR NEW LIFE IN CHRIST IS OUR GREATEST CHALLENGE. Many of us were introduced somewhere in our faith journey to the idea that we should fight against our old, nasty, selfish nature in order to grow in grace. This religious idea is not the teaching of Scripture but the concoction of those who think that sinful behavior and thinking can be overcome by fighting our selfish old nature and its desires! This is fruitless, leading us to a life of constant failure and little or no spiritual growth. Often lecturing or preaching has majored on the theme of fighting our old nature. True victory over a lifetime is not the result of rededications; but a daily walk, one step at a time, by faith, feeding the new nature on God's love, grace, and truth from the Scriptures empowered by the Holy Spirit.

The Scripture does not refer to believers as good or bad, but rather weak or strong! In any given time frame we can find ourselves both weak and strong. Victory is found in our lives one minute at a time as we walk by faith, not by feelings, which come and go and are often driven by our hormones! Humbly, one moment at a time, we learn to seek God's presence and power in our walk, feeding ourselves on God's promises and provisions. The life of faith is not built on our PERFORMANCE but GOD'S PROVISION.

A daily quiet time, a moment of thanksgiving and prayer and readings from Scripture, feed our spiritual inner man. Fighting our old selfish nature in a human, fleshly manner assures us of failure. Over a lifetime we daily face our "inability" discovering time and again that FEEDING THE NEW NATURE is indeed the way to moment by moment victory. This is never a constant beating up of the flesh, fighting our urges and failing; guilt-ridden and shamed by our inability and repeat offenses. Thus, it is daily feeding our new "in Christ" relationship, confessing our sins, and declaring thanks to God, who gives us the victory through our Lord Jesus Christ. JESUS NOT ME-SUS!

UNHINGED: Jesus looking at the multitude said they were cast down and He had compassion on them. Cast down is akin to a useless "unstrung bow." No doubt the world we live in manifests the same reality. In the language of the day we might well describe mankind in its lostness as UNHINGED. That is disordered, disoriented, or distraught. Sin reflects each of those things and reveals brokenness, a coming up short in the human condition. Scripture declares, "All have sinned." The word "sin" has been trivialized into a do or don't do routine. In truth it is a "darkness" that blinds one completely. Someone described mankind without God as a blind man in a dark room looking for a black cat. This is a true picture of lostness and being UNHINGED in a culture that lives in and loves darkness.

DARKNESS SELLS! God's love and grace as light illuminates the blight of darkness like bugs that live under a rock in darkness. When the rock is moved they flee. As did Adam and Eve in the Garden of Eden when they disobeyed God and were naked, afraid and hid. Sin is a rebellion against God and His love and care which we all have experienced. Naked in the sense that we stand with our guilt revealed, and we seek to hide out for fear of being caught. I have been there and it is a terrible place to be and it is true darkness and lostness. THANK GOD THAT JESUS, THE LIGHT OF THE WORLD, CAME TO SEEK AND TO SAVE THE LOST, AS GOD SOUGHT ADAM AND EVE AFTER THEIR REBELLION. I AM SO GLAD GOD SEEKS ME OUT AND FINDS ME WHEN I AM UNHINGED, HIDING AND AFRAID!

Thus Jesus declared of the world in the natural as "mankind loving darkness because their deeds are evil." It takes little energy to produce darkness. In the day to day world producing light is costly. God, in the domain of the Spirit, is the author of light. Dark moods, thoughts and actions emanate from the mind and heart of mankind answering to no one but themselves. Out of that darkness comes the language and actions of an anger often expressed in declaring God's last name as "damn" among other expressions that reveal meanness, hate and the UNHINGED LIFESTYLE.

While visiting a large cavern years ago we entered into its bowels. The Ranger turned the lights out ordering us not to move as we were engulfed in a darkness you could feel. He struck a single match and illuminated the massive room. Jesus died, was buried and raised from the dead to offer mankind the LIGHT of God's love and grace. THEREFORE I HAVE IN THIS DARK, UNHINGED WORLD DETERMINED TO STRIKE A MATCH RATHER THAN CURSE THE DARK. JESUS NOT ME-SUS

We live in a world of broken promises and lies attached to the letters BS. Those letters are used to echo disappointment, hurt, pain, broken dreams, lies, betrayal, deceptions, schemes and a multitude of other religious UNHINGED UNTRUTHS! Jesus confronted the BS'ers of His day who B-blindly S-suffocated the people with religious laws they themselves didn't keep. From a child I heard BS fall off the tongues of others even before I understood the anger life could bring to me, revealed by this simple verbal expression, while dealing with the unacceptable. I now know its meaning and how well it defines a moment of expressed frustration.

We often are confronted by lying politicians, preachers and teachers of error, self-appointed philosophers who distort the truth and ordinary folks who have been misled or believed a lie. THANK GOD THERE IS AN EXCHANGE for those POTENT LETTERS which often expresses our outrage either outwardly or inwardly. At 16 years of age my life was invaded by my B-Beloved S-Savior. This was not religion nor arrogant piety but a personal relationship with JESUS CHRIST!

A wonderful exchange of an angry, rebellious heart for B-Blessed S-Salvation was not bought or wrought, but a gift of God's righteousness. As a believer dealing with the war within my old nature there is another BS exchange which empowers our life and feeds our inner man. The ultimate weapon for daily strength and wisdom in our life is B-Bible S-Study. This is a lifetime pursuit that daily changes our lives. Wisdom and strength come by way of the Blessed Scriptures keeping us from failing and empowering us to grow in grace.

My first speech teacher in college was "old school" and she demanded when I made speeches in class that I not use notes. "Mr. Griffin when you speak never use notes but be filled with your subject so as to speak out of the overflow, looking into the eyes of your hearers," truly B-believer S-speak. Thus, our preparation to speak to others is to prepare ourselves by our daily walk and study of the Word. Out of the overflow of the mind and heart we will be B-battle S-strong and prepared to stand and give a reason of the hope within us.

Finally, each believer is under command to share God's grace becoming a B-Blessed S-Sower of God's

Word as His B-Bond S-Servant. THE MIRACLE OF GRACE IS AVAILABLE TO ALL, HAVING TRANSFORMED US AS BELIEVERS BY THE DEATH, BURIAL AND RESURRECTION OF JESUS CHRIST. He has EMPOWERED US as B-Burden S-Sharers IN A BROKEN, HURTING WORLD, DAILY CHOOSING TO LIGHT A CANDLE RATHER THAN CURSING THE DARK. AMAZING GRACE HOW SWEET THE SOUND! RIGHT CHOICE! JESUS NOT ME-SUS! I am then empowered by true BS / Blessed Scripture!

ACT 5

Life is indeed a journey, unpredictable as the wind and often filled with mystery and adventure, comedy and tragedy. It is never boring unless we bog down in the process and lose our way. OUR LIVES AND OUR JOURNEY IS A DRAMA THAT DEFIES DESCRIPTION THOUGH IN THIS SHORT BOOK I HAVE SOUGHT TO DEFINE IN FIVE ACTS THE HOPE WE HAVE IN A HURTING WORLD! OUR RELATIONSHIP IS WITH GOD NOT RELIGION!

The word "lost" defines man without a purpose, direction, or compass to lead him/her. When one becomes a believer in the Lord Jesus Christ on the basis of faith by grace's empowerment, he/she discovers a whole new world that God ordained. As we face the different chapters of our journey as a believer we daily pray that we would be always "surprised by joy" and our inner man strengthened by grace to His honor and glory. Each individual believer is special, the product of many influences and people that compose our lives. There are five major concerns that form our individuality, our sexuality and spirituality!

CHEMISTRY – The genetic formula that formed us is composed of many factors, some known and some unknown. Our personal DNA is comprised of our ancestry that carries certain genes forward, often skipping generations and manifesting certain abilities that were not seen in recent generations of a family. Also the mother and father bring their own particular and peculiar genes that compose a whole new person with potentials, strengths and weaknesses. It perhaps takes a lifetime to discover all that is within us. We have nothing at all to do with this, but it is the gift of our parents to us. While in the womb our mothers hopefully contributed to our health and our physical future by her faithful pursuit of proper diet and life style. Even attitude and a loving environment transmit to the womb. There can be exceptions and mutations which affect and infect certain persons!

CONDITIONING - The second factor that contributes to our journey and forms our first ways of thinking about everything, is conditioning. During our first years we pick up on so many ways of thinking about life, our sexuality, spirituality, life style, boundaries and how we understand right and wrong. This will continue into our teen years, young adulthood and our senior years. The die is cast. God can alter the course once it is set. Thoughts begin to fill and condition our once blank tape. Emotional responses to every day experiences and family affect who we are and eventually who we become and how we will respond to life situations. Conditioning is the one factor that will continually confront us over a lifetime and affect how we respond to life situations. The knowledge of God and His authority, present or absent, conditions our self-hood as no other issue, especially concerning the meaning and ultimate purpose of life.

CULTURE – It doesn't take a rocket scientist to see how we all have been greatly influenced by our culture. As I have traveled the world over, I have seen time and again that each culture displays itself through its children. Certain patterns are repeated and manifested generation after generation, setting up traditions and forms of morality or immorality peculiar to its own culture. I am reminded daily that this culture today is not the culture I grew up with.

CIRCUMSTANCES - As we move from childhood into adolescence and adulthood and deal with the reality of personal pain and emotional hurt, we handle life's circumstances by falling back on the process lived out by our family and peers. Here again is the need to have a personal relationship with God and a "faith force" to view life through His plan and purpose for our lives and move beyond our initial conditioning and the surrounding culture to cope with life's ups and downs. Every person has their share of the good, the bad and the ugly, but it is how we deal with it that makes the difference. We must remember that "The God of the mountain top is also the God of the valley and He is always sufficient." We have many questions and there are no bad questions but many bad answers and as believers we learn to filter those answers through COMMON SENSE AND **B-Blessed S-Scriptures!**

CHOICES – The bottom line in the chain of influences on our lives is our personal choices. No doubt other influences carry weight, but the final matter is our choices. Love is a choice, happiness is a choice, life is the sum total of our choices. Our spirituality is a work of God's love and grace, a gift of His righteousness. Our reception of this great miracle of love is a CHOICE. We all have made choices that hurt us and led down dead end streets. Jesus and the scriptures call us to make a choice.

There are some choices that are once in a lifetime, but most choices come in the daily process and often are repetitive in nature, demanding that we "trust the Lord, acknowledging Him in all our ways." We must remember that life isn't a spectator sport but a continual, day by day interaction with light and darkness, righteousness and evil. In Christ, we have "His righteousness a gift," thus it is about Him working in and through us, "Christ in us the hope of glory." It is always JESUS NOT ME-SUS! Charlotte Elliott, (1789-1871) wrote the following lines from the song "Just As I Am" which declares my feelings that night at sixteen as I understood the message of God's grace as my very own:

"Just as I am, though tossed about
With many a conflict, many a doubt,
Fightings and fears within, without,
O Lamb of God, I come, I come."

Over the years I had rebelled against the term "good and bad Christian." I grew to understand that no such reality existed, nor is it a Biblical concept. This is a turn off to anyone who might consider the claims of Christ. The truth of Scripture is a matter of "weak and strong" which can be realized in a believer at any time. The very reality of Jesus Christ in our lives sets up a conflict between our old "carnal" nature and the "righteousness of God" which brings salvation and options of an eternal nature. He declared "the just shall live by faith." The natural man has no such struggle, "not understanding the things of God," nor its work in his or her life.

As a pastor's son and "church kid" I came to think, that I wanted to be a "good Christian," so as to be truly religious and proper among the people who called the plays in my life. It didn't take me long to realize that being good was not my thing. The Scripture declares that "none are good" and that our righteousness is as a "filthy rag." Thus I learned to "act like a Christian" whatever that was thought to be, determined by the group I was in at the time. I really learned to be an actor and a poor one at that. After a personal interaction with the Gospel and grace at the age of sixteen I began to search the Scriptures for myself. I discovered I was never commanded to be good and not bad. Good was used for deeds and works toward others, not my own doing.

Goodness is a fruit of the Spirit of God by which we as believers are empowered to do "good works"! Eventually, "Spiritual Maintenance" would come from a verse which commanded to "maintain good works for they are good and profitable for men"! No command to do them to gain approval of God but to impact others. I discovered that there were no bad questions but that I had been given bad answers from which Scripture began to set me free. I began to grasp the truth that believers deal with being weak because of our connection to our flesh nature and strong as relates to the work of the Holy Spirit who lives within the believer.

Thus, the hard reality is that our flesh is vulnerable and weak while our inner man is enabled by the Holy Spirit to be strong. We are "born to war." Self-righteousness has no place in the life of the believer but when we posture and create the appearance of piety and being a "goodie two-shoes or holy Joe" we fool ourselves and disconnect from hurting, unbelieving people and other believers. Paul the apostle declared that when he was weak, he was strong.

When we become all things to all men that we might win them, we must have bigger ears and a smaller mouth, humbly walking in big shoes. Our holiness is our "wholeness empowered by the Holy Spirit" as "temples of the Holy Spirit" who lives within us. The "God's house" in this world is each believer in-dwelt and empowered by the Spirit. God does not live in buildings made with hands, period. We are "God's house," we are the "church."

No one can destroy the faith of Jesus Christ, but they can well destroy a religious Christianity not connected to a living faith in Jesus Christ! Jesus did not come to start a religion but rather to fulfill the covenant of Jehovah established in creation, in Adam and Eve, in Noah, and transferred to Abraham and his seed forever. A living faith that rested in the promise and fulfillment of God's Covenant with man on the basis of faith, period! The Lord Jesus Christ came into the world in a baby's skin, born of a virgin, died, buried and rose from the dead that we might have everlasting life and here and now "life abundantly."

Thus, the "gift of GOD'S righteousness" is a gift to all who will trust Him. It is freely given and we receive His love and grace by faith alone. We can now on the basis of faith declare we are an imperfect, greatly loved, and forgiven child of God. We are sometimes weak and sometimes strong but never good or bad. Jesus Christ came to seek and find people like you and me while we were yet sinners, dead in trespasses and sin. He came to die for us, to live in us and to use us for His glory and our good.

In a world of talking heads and faceless crowds, the world of religion has become a consumer item. Its leadership has often become CEO minded rather than servant driven. The life of faith is one of "Closet Power," and "Christ in Us," is the hope of glory. The world of religion often develops a cosmetic, plastic piety overdosed on meeting attendance and sermon sampling. Jesus Christ came to reveal God's love for all mankind without partiality. He came to seek and to save all mankind revealing their lostness, and offering His righteousness as a gift of love and grace. His death, burial and resurrection are the heart of the Gospel of grace. He calls us to a life of humility and "Closet PRAYER Power"!

Jesus did not come to start a mass movement or win the world to Himself by corporate gimmicks and appeals. God throughout human history, chose to use the power of one man or woman to address his or her world. Masses have indeed come to the simple message of the cross and resurrection, but discipleship demands a walk, up-close and personal. Jesus Christ always attached Himself to individuals revealing Himself in such a way that each human encounter built a personal relationship.

We are never commanded to go to church but instructed in how to be the church. Jesus declared, "He that is the greatest among you is servant of all." Jesus declared, "They will know that you are my disciples because you love one another." Anothering is the application of "agape love" that is an unconditional love that reaches out to the brokenness of believer and unbeliever alike until they are drawn to the Father.

The local gathering of believers should never be defined by denomination or personality, but by its reason for being. Ministry, fellowship and study with one another should not only define us but describe us. It is only through "Closet Power" that this kind of force and usefulness can be constant. We live in a culture that talks about someone coming out of the closet. Usually it implies some kind of sexual matter just revealed. We as believers need to come out of the closet for Jesus, not religion.

Being identified with Christ versus the many flavors of Christianity is a wonderful thing. Christianity and self-declared Christians with their many differing beliefs and dogmas often prove a turn off! Those of us who follow Jesus in the Scriptures discover a different Jesus. Paul declared that, "we should make it our ambition to live a quiet life, mind our own business and work with our hands."

Peter declares that we should "sanctify the Lord in our hearts and be ready to give a reason of our hope to THOSE WHO ASK…"!

"BE CAREFUL TO MAINTAIN GOOD WORKS, FOR THEY ARE GOOD AND PROFITABLE FOR MANKIND."

"LET YOUR LIGHT SO SHINE AMONG MANKIND THAT THEY WILL SEE YOUR GOOD WORKS AND GLORIFY YOUR FATHER WHICH IS IN HEAVEN."

JESUS NOT ME-SUS!

THE GOSPEL OF JESUS CHRIST IS NOT ABOUT HELL BUT HOPE! A drowning man does not need a lecture on life or death. An example of swimming strokes is a mockery to his reality. A textbook thrown to him only adds a burden to his condition. The only HOPE he has is to be plucked from his impossible dilemma. Any other option is certain death! The work of God, Jesus said, was "to believe Him who God sent," a reference to Himself.

The Gospel is that Jesus, died, was buried and rose from the dead to give us life everlasting. Lecturing mankind on sin, heaven, hell, and the grave does not proclaim the Gospel! Scripture declares that the Holy Spirit alone convicts the world of sin, righteousness and judgment. Jesus delivered his message of judgement to the self-righteous, religious leaders.

The greatest problem of the unbeliever is his/her unbelief by default declares their righteousness equal to God's and if there is no God then man's righteousness can be an extension of him/her lifestyle. Jesus spoke of those who could destroy the soul in hell. His address of hell was in context of those who maintained a context of "good works" which magnified their pride, engendering "hypocrisy" which we have each one encountered in our own lives.

Self-righteousness is the rejection of God, His LOVE and grace. God sends no one to hell, but man's arrogant idolatry separates him from God. The travesty is, though hell is eternal separation from God, mankind's separation from God during the days of his earthly journey which is filled with self-righteous hopelessness! The Scriptures declare THAT JESUS THE CHRIST DID NOT COME INTO THE WORLD TO DAMN OR CONDEMN THE WORLD, BUT THAT THE WORLD THROUGH HIM MIGHT BE SAVED. Christ in YOU the HOPE of glory!
JESUS NOT ME-SUS

LIFE IS SHORT!
DEATH IS SURE!
SIN THE CAUSE!
JESUS CHRIST THE CURE!
**THE MOMENT I TRUSTED
LORD JESUS CHRIST**

- I became a child of God – John 1:12
- I was chosen of God and born by His will – Ephesians 1:2, John 1:13
- My sins past, present and future were forgiven – Romans 4:7-8, 2 Corinthians 5:21

- I became an heir of God and joint heir with Jesus Christ – Romans 5:9
- I was saved from the wrath of God – Romans 5:9
- I was reckoned righteous – Romans 4, 5, 6
- I received eternal life – John 5:24, I John 5:13
- I was guaranteed no condemnation – John 5:24, Romans 8:1
- I was reconciled to God – 2 Corinthians 5:18
- I was justified and given peace with God – Romans 5:1-2
- I was born again of incorruptible seed – I Peter 1:23
- I was delivered from the power of darkness and redeemed – Colossians 1:13-14
- I was made a new creation, now in Christ forever – 2 Corinthians 5:17
- I was sanctified and perfected forever – I Corinthians 1:30, Hebrews 10:10, 14
- I was made complete in Christ – Colossians 2:8-15
- I was born of the Spirit, my body is His temple – John 3:16, I Corinthians 6:19-20
- I was baptized in the Holy Spirit – I Corinthians 12:13
- I was indwelt by the Holy Spirit – John 14:16-17, Romans 8:9
- I was sealed by the Holy Spirit – Ephesians 1:13-14, 4:30

- I became a citizen of heaven – Ephesians 2:19, Philippians 3:20
- I am His workmanship – Ephesians 2:20
- I am made able to walk in the newness of life – Romans 6:4
- I am no longer a forced slave of sin – Romans 6:6-7
- I was the recipient of God's free gift – Romans 6:23, Ephesians 2:8-9
- I was enabled to bear fruit for God – Romans 7:4
- I was enabled to serve in the newness of Spirit – Romans 7:6
- I was set free from the law of sin and death – Romans 8:2
- I was enabled to please God – Romans 8:5-9
- I now belong to Christ and was made spiritually alive in Him – Romans 8:9-10
- I am unable to be separated from the love of God – Romans 8:35-39

GROWING IN JESUS CHRIST
TRUST & OBEY

✓ Be devoted to ONE another … Romans 12:10
✓ Give preference to ONE another… Romans 12:10
✓ Be of the same mind toward ONE another…Romans 12:16
✓ Love ONE another…Romans 13:8

- ✓ Accept ONE another…Romans 15:7
- ✓ Admonish ONE another…Roman 15:14
- ✓ Care for ONE another…I Corinthians 12:25
- ✓ Serve ONE another…Galatians 5:13
- ✓ Bear ONE another's burdens…Galatians 6:2
- ✓ Show patience to ONE another…Ephesians 4:1-4
- ✓ Be kind to ONE another…Ephesians 4:32
- ✓ Do not lie to ONE another…Colossians 3:9
- ✓ Bear with ONE another…Colossians 3:12-13
- ✓ Teach and admonish ONE another…Colossians 3:16
- ✓ Comfort ONE another…I Thessalonians 4:18
- ✓ Encourage ONE another…Hebrews 3:13
- ✓ Stimulate ONE another to love and good deeds…Hebrews 10:23
- ✓ Pray for ONE another…James 5:16
- ✓ Do not speak against ONE another…James 4:11
- ✓ Do not complain…against ONE another…James 5:9
- ✓ CLOTHE YOURSELVES WITH HUMILITY TOWARD ONE ANOTHER.

WORKS BY DANNY GRIFFIN

- **Dancing With Broken Feet**
  Dealing with the pain and pressures of marriage including divorce, remarriage, blended families and more

- **Dancing With A Broken World**
  Danny takes his knowledge from decades of walking with the Lord and weds Biblical truth with practical living.

- **Dancing With Jesus In A Hurting World**
  Danny uplifts and encourages the true believer and follower of Christ to be God's ambassadorial mission in today's culture and world.

- **Dancing With Grace Amazing**
  The word GRACE is used 159 times in Scripture. Danny defines and explores this astounding concept.

- **Dancing With A Broken Me**
  Danny personalizes his walk with the LORD and strives to answer the question, "Who are you really, pilgrim?"

- **Jesus Not Me-sus**
  Relationship vs. Religion

For information on how to obtain any of the above visit:

http://www.SpiritualMaintenance.org/books.html

Made in the USA
Columbia, SC
02 June 2019